THE LAMP

A PLAY IN ONE ACT

Melville Lovatt

TSL Drama

Dedication

To my brother, Ken.

By Melville Lovatt

Full Length Plays

Small Mercies	Comedy-Drama	4M	2F
The Powers That Be	Thriller	3M	2F
Visiting Time	Family Drama	3M	2F
Desperate Measures	Dark Comedy	3M	1F

One Act Plays

Accommodation	Tragicomedy	4M	1F
The Lamp	Comedy-Drama	1M	1F
The Distressed Table	Comedy-Drama	1M	1F + Voiceover (F)
The Boomerang	Comedy-Drama	3M	1Boy + Voiceover (F)
Making Adjustments	Comedy-Drama	1M	2F
The Kiss	Thriller	2M	1F
The Weekend	Drama	2M	1F
The Grave	Drama	2M	
Bus Stop Blues			
4 Short Comedy-Drama Sketches		1M 1F, 2F, 2M, 2M	
2 Monologues	Comedy-Drama	1M, 1M	

Duologue

Bedtime Story	Drama	1M	1F

Monologue Collections

Standing Alone	Comedy-Drama	8M	8F
(16 monologues)			

All enquiries to TSL Publications: www.tslbooks.uk

The Lamp

A Play In One Act

was first presented as part of
The Harrow Festival
by
Belmont Theatre Company
on
13 July 2005
at
The Travellers Studio Theatre, Harrow Arts Centre,

with the following cast.

Arnold	**Bernard Vick**
Doreen	**Esme Tyers**
Directed	**Melville Lovatt**

Running Time

35 minutes

Characters

DOREEN: *a woman in her early sixties*

ARNOLD: *a man in his early sixties*

Setting

A medium sized display room belonging to a large second hand furniture shop.

An open doorway, CB, leads out to a larger unseen area, rear.

The door itself is operated from the rear and remains out of view until closed.

The room is used to display smaller furniture.

The goods are generally of very mixed quality, arranged in a semi-circle.

Stretching outwards from the back wall, along both sides.

Assorted bric-a-brac.

An old record player, towards rear, L.

Two china umbrella stands, towards rear, R.

A medium sized sofa bed, SC.

DL, on a table, a lamp.

Author's Production Note

For One Act Play Festivals and similar events, the above set can be suggested by the players, leaving only the sofa bed visible.

If suggested, the lamp and door should be distanced, door towards front, overlooking auditorium.

SET DIAGRAM
(For bare minimum set, props in dashed lines can be suggested by the players)

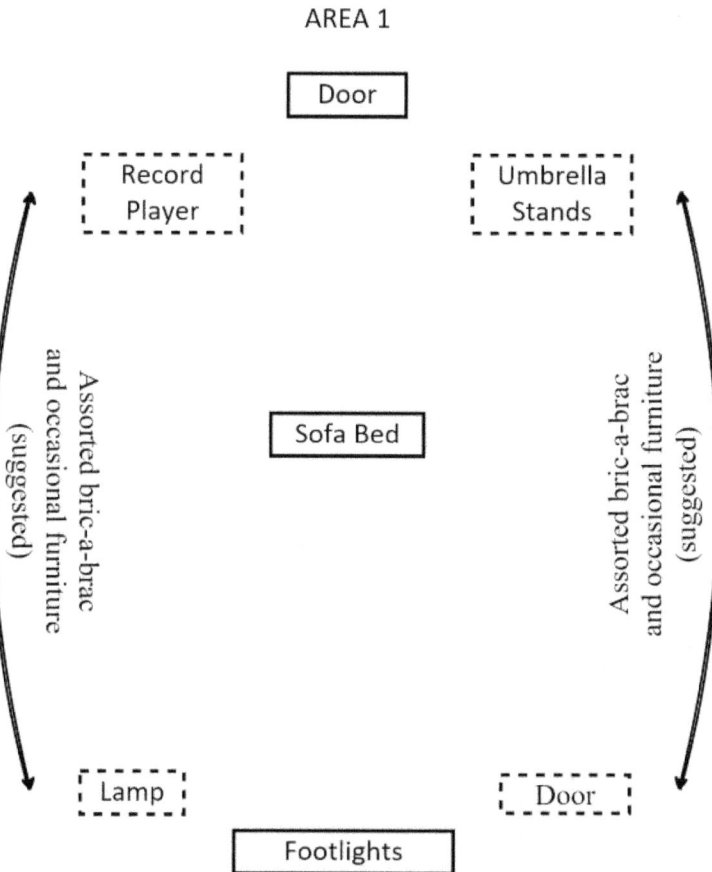

AREA 1

| Door |

| Record Player | | Umbrella Stands |

Assorted bric-a-brac and occasional furniture (suggested)

| Sofa Bed |

Assorted bric-a-brac and occasional furniture (suggested)

| Lamp | | Door |

| Footlights |

Late Sunday afternoon. DOREEN *and* ARNOLD *stand, staring at the lamp which gives off a soft, subdued light.*
ARNOLD *wears a raincoat.*

> *Silence.*

DOREEN: (*Sighs, shakes her head.*) I know it's nice. I agree that it's nice. The thing is, will it go? With the stuff that we've got?

> *Pause.*

I don't think it will go. Do you think it will?

> *Pause.*

I don't think it will.

> *Pause.*

ARNOLD: Let's be off, then.

DOREEN: Wait.

ARNOLD: Let's give it a miss.

DOREEN: Let's just ... think about it.

ARNOLD: We already have.

DOREEN: You think it will go, then?

ARNOLD: Doreen, I ... look ...

DOREEN: If you think it will go ...

ARNOLD: No. Oh no. No, I'm not having that. I'm not taking the blame if you're not happy with it. No way. No. I'd sooner just leave it. Forget it. Okay?

DOREEN: (*Examines lamp, closely.*) I do rather like it.

ARNOLD: (*Sighs wearily.*) Buy it, then.

DOREEN: (*Slow, considers.*) Well …

ARNOLD: Look, Doreen. Listen, we can't stay here all day.

(*Glances at watch.*) What time does he close here, anyway?

Eh? Look, it's Sunday, remember? It's four-thirty now.

DOREEN: He'll be here until six.

ARNOLD: Not on Sunday, he won't.

DOREEN: Well, he's in no rush to get rid of us, is he? *Is he?*

(*Points, peering through doorway.*) Look. He's still sitting at his desk. He's still reading his newspaper.

He looks half asleep. No, he's in no rush. No rush at all.

Pause.

(*Peering through doorway.*) What a big shop this is.

Such a big rambling place. There're little rooms everywhere … all branching off. It's enormous, really.

ARNOLD: Enormous and bleak.

DOREEN: From the magazine, I thought it was just fairly small.

ARNOLD: Can we make a decision? A final decision?

Can we just make a decision and go?

DOREEN: What do *you* think?

ARNOLD: I've told you. You know what I think.

DOREEN: I'm not sure …

ARNOLD: Let's leave it, then. If you're not sure.

DOREEN: It might … might fit in. Then again, it might not.

ARNOLD: This is getting us no nowhere. Nowhere.

DOREEN: (*Decisive.*) Right. I've got it.

ARNOLD: What?

DOREEN: The answer.

ARNOLD: Eh?

DOREEN: We'll just ask him if we can take the lamp home.

Take it home on approval. That way, we'll know.

We'll know straightaway once we get it in the room.

(*Peers through doorway.*) Do you think he'll agree to it?

ARNOLD: *I* don't agree. Look, Doreen, we're talking twenty-five miles! If the lamp's not right, then I bring it back?

That's what you're suggesting?

DOREEN: At least we'd be sure.

ARNOLD: Well, I'm sure. I'm sure I'm not doing it. Right?

DOREEN: I'm more or less certain it will be alright ...

ARNOLD: We've been in here an hour. A whole bloody hour!

DOREEN: There's no need to swear.

ARNOLD: You're making me swear!

DOREEN: Alright. Calm down. I think it will go.

ARNOLD: Let's get it, then.

DOREEN: Oh, there's a chip on it.

ARNOLD: What?

DOREEN: There's a chip on it. Look. I didn't spot it before.

It's the light. The light's in this room's very bad.

ARNOLD: Where's the chip?

DOREEN: On the edge.

ARNOLD: (*Examines lamp, closely.*) I can't see it.

DOREEN: (*Points.*) There. Just *there.*

ARNOLD: (*Incredulous.*) That's nothing!

DOREEN: *I* noticed it. Right? In our room, with the light, we'll notice it more.

ARNOLD: (*Starts to move off.*) That's it, then. Let's leave it.

DOREEN: You think it's nothing?

ARNOLD: (*Weary.*) Does it matter what I think, Doreen?

DOREEN: Of course.

ARNOLD: Well, I do think it's nothing. It can just be touched up.

          Touched up with a pen. You can buy special pens.

          Touch up pens.

DOREEN: Really?

ARNOLD: I could just ... touch it up. You wouldn't notice it, then.

DOREEN: Can you guarantee that?

ARNOLD: (*Sighs.*) No, I can't ... guarantee it.

DOREEN: Not worth it, then. No. No, I'd just be aware of it all of the time. It would bother me. Bug me.

ARNOLD: Then there's no point.

DOREEN: (*Looks at lamp, closely.*) It is only slight, though ...

ARNOLD: (*End of tether.*) Doreen ...

DOREEN: (*Nods.*) No point.

ARNOLD: (*Turns to go.*) We're agreed, then. We leave it.

          We leave it. Okay? We're agreed. We leave it. Right?

DOREEN: (*Turns to go.*) Right.

ARNOLD: That's final?

DOREEN: Final.

ARNOLD: Let's get something to eat. There's a pub across the road that … (*Discovers the door is now closed.*)

Hello, what's this? (*Small chuckle.*) Don't tell me we're locked in. That's all we need.

(*Tries door.*) Bloody hell! We are! We bloody well are!

(*Shouts.*) Open up! We're still in here!

(*Bangs hard on door.*) Open up! Don't believe it!

The dozy sod's locked us both in!

(*Bangs on door.*) Hello! Hello!

DOREEN: Oh my God, he's gone home. He's locked up and gone home.

ARNOLD: Don't panic. Alright? Open up! We're still in here!

Open up! Open up! Open up!

DOREEN: Hello! Hello!

ARNOLD: Open up! We're still in here! Open up! We're still in here!

BOTH TOGETHER: OPEN UP!

Pause.

DOREEN: What'll we do?

ARNOLD: Have to break down the door.

DOREEN: Think we can?

ARNOLD: (*Doubtful, shakes head.*) It's like a fire door …

DOREEN: (*Looks around.*) There's no other way. There're no windows.

ARNOLD: Christsake! God what a prat! What a stupid dickhead!

ARNOLD *kicks the door, hard, then winces, groans, clutches foot.*

Aaaahh! Aaaahh!

ARNOLD *sits, grimacing, rubbing his foot.*

DOREEN: (*Bangs on door.*) Hello! Are you there? Cooee! Cooee!

ARNOLD: (*Groans.*) Oh my God.

DOREEN: (*Stern.*) Open up now! Do you hear?!

ARNOLD: (*Whimpers.*) I've broken my toes. I've broken my toes.

DOREEN: If they were broken, you'd be in agony.

ARNOLD: I *am* in agony!

DOREEN: (*Bangs on door.*) Open up! Hello! Hello!

Blackout.

Lights up. Lamp on. Subdued lighting as before.

DOREEN *and* ARNOLD *sitting on sofa bed.*

> *Pause.*

DOREEN: *(Gets up, paces back and forth.)* So what do we do? Just sit here and wait until he opens tomorrow?

> *Pause.*

Is that what we do?

ARNOLD: That's all we *can* do.

> *Pause.*

What else can we do?

DOREEN: Well ... we can make some more noise.

ARNOLD: We've made lots of noise. Nobody can hear us.

These walls are too thick. These walls are as thick as Fort bloody Knox.

> *Pause.*

God. What a mess.

> *Pause.*

(Stands, paces.) I just can't comprehend how anyone can be so damned stupid. It beggars belief!

I mean, it's common sense, isn't it? Before you lock up, you check to see nobody's left inside! *(Shrugs.)* He just must have been dreaming. In a world of his own.

He must have been in a complete bloody trance.

Just wait 'til I see him. He won't know what's hit him. I'll have his head on a platter for this.

DOREEN: Calm down.

ARNOLD: Calm down?

DOREEN: Your blood pressure, dear. He's not worth you getting into a state.

ARNOLD: Yes, you're right. You're right. We have to stay calm.

Pause.

We must stay calm.

Pause.

(*Suddenly remembers.*) Ah!

DOREEN: Ah, what?

ARNOLD: Your phone!

DOREEN: What?

ARNOLD: The phone I've just bought you. Your new i-phone!

DOREEN: I didn't bring it.

ARNOLD: Didn't bring it?

DOREEN: I didn't think I'd need it. I just didn't feel like humping it around.

ARNOLD: (*Explodes.*) But it's tiny! It's tiny! Your phone is tiny! Just why do you think they made it so small?

So you don't have to *hump* it. Just pop it in your pocket.

What could be simpler? What could be ... look, you pestered me stupid for a new bloody phone. You pestered me, didn't you?

Week after week?

(*Mimics her voice.*) All my friends have got an i-phone. All except me.

Then you don't bloody use it! Tell me the point!

DOREEN: The point is I simply forgot it. Alright? I simply forgot it.

(*Barks, bangs on door.*) Hello! Open up!

ARNOLD: Nobody can hear. There's nobody there.

DOREEN: (*Angrily.*) Open up!

ARNOLD: You're wasting your time.

Blackout.

Lights up as before.

ARNOLD *and* DOREEN *sitting on sofa bed.*

They both stare ahead.

Pause.

DOREEN: Arnold?

ARNOLD: What?

DOREEN: Supposing …

ARNOLD: What?

DOREEN: Supposing he doesn't come tomorrow?

ARNOLD: He will.

DOREEN: I wish *I* felt so sure.

ARNOLD: Of course he'll come.

Pause.

DOREEN: Supposing he doesn't?

ARNOLD: (*Impatient, produces magazine cutting.*) Look. Here's the advert.

It says he trades six days a week. He just closes on Wednesdays.

DOREEN: (*Sceptical.*) Not Mondays?

ARNOLD: No! It says Wednesday. Read it. Just read it.

(*Hands her the cutting.*) Here. For Godsake, let's not make this worse than it is. He'll be open tomorrow at ten o'clock. Right?

DOREEN: If you say so.

ARNOLD: I *do* say so.

DOREEN: (*Stabs at cutting with finger.*) What about this?
(*Reads from cutting.*) Open *some* Bank Holidays.
Please ring to check. (*Handing cutting back.*)
Tomorrow's Bank Holiday Monday.

ARNOLD: (*Alarmed, snatches cutting.*) What?

DOREEN: Open *some* Bank Holidays. Please ring to check.
He might be open. Then again, he might not.

ARNOLD closes eyes, slumps forward, head in hands.

He looks up, stares blankly ahead.

ARNOLD: Why did we come here? All this way for a stupid
lamp.

DOREEN: It wasn't *just* that. You wanted to see the cathedral,
you said. A nice drive, you said. It was all your idea.

ARNOLD: (*Waves magazine cutting at her.*) If you hadn't seen
the lamp in this bloody magazine ...

DOREEN: Oh, what does it matter? We're here.

Pause. They both stare ahead.

I suppose I could pray.

ARNOLD: Pray?

DOREEN: Say a prayer.

ARNOLD: A prayer?

DOREEN: Pray he opens tomorrow.

Pause.

You could say one as well.

ARNOLD: There's nobody listening. You're wasting your time.

(*Looks up.*) There's no one up there.

DOREEN: Well, supposing there is someone up there and you have to go before him on Judgement Day, eh?

I mean, what on earth will he think about you?

You've been saying all your life that he doesn't exist.

So when you go before him, what will he think?

Pause.

ARNOLD: I think this God would welcome me in. He'd welcome me in with open arms.

He'd say to himself, this guy's really something!

These believers never stop pestering my at all.

Always asking for something. Day in, day out.

This guy here, he's never asked me for anything!

Never troubled me since the day he was born!

Come in! He'd shout to me. Come in, my son!

Welcome to my Kingdom Of Heaven!

DOREEN: Oh, you're so smart, aren't you? So smug and smart?

You'll choke on your own stupid wit.

Pause.

DOREEN: God, I'm hungry now. And it's gonna get worse.

Pause.

Have you got any mints?

Pause.

Have you got any mints?

ARNOLD: You had the last one.

DOREEN: I thought you bought two packets.

ARNOLD: No. Only one.

~ 20 ~

DOREEN: And you've gobbled them up? I only had two.

Pause.

Not even a mint.

Pause.

It wouldn't be so bad if there was something to read.

A book or a newspaper. Anything just ... just to take your mind off ... (*Shrugs.*) help pass the time ...

Pause.

Something to read.

Pause.

Did you hear about the nurse, yesterday?

The nurse on trial for murder?

Pause.

There's this nurse on trial. A hospital nurse.

She went round the ward, unplugging machines.

First she unplugged an old man, then went on from there.

Like a spree. Unplugging everything in sight.

All the terminal cases. She unplugged about ten.

Well, she said she was doing them all a good turn.

She was shortening their suffering. Shortening their pain.

Pause.

The jury's still out.

Pause.

Arnold?

ARNOLD: What?

DOREEN: Will you promise me something?

ARNOLD: Mmn?

DOREEN: Just promise me?

ARNOLD: Promise you what?

DOREEN: If I ever become ... if I ever become ... well, *ill* ... very ill ... like, a terminal case ... if I ever become like a cabbage, you'll just ...

ARNOLD: Just what?

DOREEN: Pull the plug?

           Pause.

ARNOLD: Might as well pull it now, then.

DOREEN: Thanks very much. I'm serious.

ARNOLD: Godsake.

DOREEN: Promise me?

ARNOLD: Look ...

DOREEN: I'd do it for you. If you were a terminal case, I'd pull the plug out for you.

ARNOLD: Tell me something. What makes ... what makes you think ... what makes you think I'd want it pulled out? What makes you think I'd want the plug pulled?

DOREEN: 'Course you would.

ARNOLD: Oh really? How do you know?

DOREEN: I know you.

ARNOLD: Really?

DOREEN: You'd want it pulled out.

ARNOLD: But supposing I didn't? Supposing I didn't?

           Supposing I wanted a natural death?

           Supposing I just didn't want to be killed?

DOREEN: Killed?

ARNOLD: Murdered.

DOREEN: I wouldn't call it that.

ARNOLD: What would you call it?

DOREEN: Released from pain. (*Shrugs.*) Suit yourself.

            If it's your wish to die in pain, I'll let you.

            If that's your final request. I mean, if that's what you want.

            A lingering death. You're welcome to it.

ARNOLD: Thanks.

            Pause.

DOREEN: (*Rather lightly.*) My uncle died of cancer, aged forty-five.

            My aunt fed him. Spoon-fed him. Like a baby. Liquids only.

            Just like a child. She washed him and dressed him and wiped his bottom and watched his pride drain out of his eyes and his eyes ... eyes begged her ... *begged* her, she said. If you truly love me, you'll kill me, they said. And she couldn't ... couldn't look ... couldn't look in his eyes. If you love me, you'll kill me.

            Couldn't look in his eyes. And she watched him die.

            Die very slowly. Watched him wither. Wither away.

            In the end, there was nothing. Skin and bone.

            Pause.

            Nothing at all.

            Pause.

            (*Shrugs, casual.*) But if that's what you want ...

ARNOLD: (*Stands.*) I don't believe this. I don't believe what I'm hearing. Look...if you've finished these stories of everlasting joy, let's try and get some sleep.

Pause. He begins to take off sofa bed cushions.

DOREEN: (*Stands.*) What you doing?

ARNOLD: This is a sofa bed, right?

DOREEN: We can't sleep on that.

ARNOLD: Where else do you suggest? On the floor?

DOREEN: I mean, won't we ...?

ARNOLD: Won't we what?

DOREEN: Well ... won't we dirty it?

ARNOLD: Dirty it? (*Patient.*) Doreen, get real.

Look, in case you've forgotten, *he's* locked us both in.

We're locked in this room through no fault of our own.

Now, as far as I'm concerned, this sofa bed's ours.

DOREEN: How can it be ours?

ARNOLD: (*Opens up sofa bed.*) It's ours for the night.

I'm sure as hell not sleeping on the floor.

DOREEN: But supposing we soil it?

ARNOLD: Soil it?

DOREEN: I mean ... we've no toilet, have we?

ARNOLD: No?

Points to the china umbrella stands.

DOREEN: (*Horrified, stares at them.*) Oh, not the umbrella stands ...

ARNOLD: No choice, have we? Consider them both as chamber pots.

DOREEN: No! (*Examines umbrella stands.*) They're the finest bone china.

ARNOLD: All the better to piss in.

DOREEN: Crude. You're always so crude.

ARNOLD: (*Lies on sofa bed.*) This is really quite comfy.

            Not bad at all. Good construction. Sprung mattress.

            Not bad at all. Yes …

DOREEN: If you speak to him nicely, he'll give you a job as a salesman.

            You might as well just get a job.

ARNOLD: How'd you mean?

DOREEN: Well, let's face it, I never see you anyway.

            You're out in that shed from morning 'til night.

            What you *doing* in there?

ARNOLD: You know what I'm doing. I'm making things, aren't I?

            Things for the house.

DOREEN: But I *never* see you. Honest to God, I see less of you now than before you retired. I thought when you retired we'd see more of each other. More, not less. Oh well, silly me.

ARNOLD: Oh come on …

DOREEN: No, it's true. It's as if you're … hiding. Hiding from me.

            Out in that shed.

ARNOLD: Now you're just being stupid. Why would I hide?

DOREEN: (*Pointedly, faces him.*) Well, suppose … suppose you tell me?

Pause.

(*As* ARNOLD *turns away.*) I heard you.

Pause.

I heard you, last night. I walked pass the shed to water the plants and I heard you. Crying. I stood by the door.

Pause.

ARNOLD: (*Softly, turns away on his side of sofa bed.*) Just go to sleep.

Lights down to dim on DOREEN *and* ARNOLD.

They are both asleep, covered by ARNOLD's *coat.*

Silence.

DOREEN'S VOICEOVER: (*Slowly.*) She looks … very old. She stands by my feet.

At first she just stands … at the end of the bed.

Her head … her head's turned. She's looking outside.

Pause.

I can't see her face.

Pause.

Then she turns. Turns towards me. Looks at me. Smiles.

She moves towards me, slowly, smiling her smile.

She's holding something. Her thumb and finger holding something. Something small. Something tiny.

Glistens. Glistens in the dark.

Pause.

Can't see what it is.

Pause.

She stands. Stands over me. Stands ... quite still.

Can't see her face, clearly. She's very long hair.

Then she bends. Leans over me. Over me ... close.

Her hand ... holding something ... moves ... moves down ... moves down ... to my face ... to my eye ... my eye ... IT'S A NEEDLE! SHE'S PUSHING IT ...!

DOREEN:	(*Awakes, sits bolt upright. Screams.*) AAAAIII!
ARNOLD:	(*Badly shaken, gets up, switches on lamp.*) Christ.
DOREEN:	I'm sorry. I sorry.
ARNOLD:	Alright.
DOREEN:	I'm sorry.
ARNOLD:	Lie back, now. Just ... just relax.
DOREEN:	There was this ... this old woman. Leaning over the bed.
ARNOLD:	Who was she?
DOREEN:	Don't know. Never seen her before.
ARNOLD:	Leaning over the bed?
DOREEN:	With a needle in her hand. She was pushing it down in my eye.
ARNOLD:	Yuk. Why can't you have nice dreams, now and again?
DOREEN:	(*With irony.*) Oh, excuse me. I'm ever so sorry.
ARNOLD:	It's just ...
DOREEN:	Just what?

ARNOLD: (*Shrugs.*) They're just always … (*Small chuckle.*) Always bad dreams.

DOREEN: Not always, they're not.

ARNOLD: Nine times out of ten.

DOREEN: Once I dreamt of bluebells. Bluebells in the woods.

           We were both picking bluebells. Remember?

ARNOLD: No. Picking bluebells?

DOREEN: I told you. Long time ago, now.

ARNOLD: I've forgotten.

DOREEN: I'll refresh your memory, then. Yes. We were both in the woods. It was Whippendell Woods.

           I remember the tall silver birches and pines and the ground sloping downwards, down towards the hollow.

           The quiet and the stillness. Yes, everything still.

           It was summer. Quite hot. (*Small chuckle.*) You were wearing shorts. Oh, I know you *never ever* wear shorts, but in the dream, you were wearing them, then.

           I remember thinking you looked quite trim.

           Then you called across to me. 'Come and see this!'

           I looked up. I could just see you there through the trees.

           You were some distance from me.

           'Come here! Look at this!' You were just like a schoolboy.

           So excited. 'Come here! Come here! Come here! Look at this!'

           When I knelt by your side, you were holding a bird.

~ 28 ~

A tiny robin with an injured foot.

'We'll take him home with us.' That's what you said.

'We'll nurse him better.' That's what we did. We took him home with us. Nursed him better. Looked after him. Fed him.

One day he was gone. But whilst he was there, he brought us ... closer?

ARNOLD *turns off the lamp.*

At any rate, *one* nice dream.

ARNOLD *lies down again, his back to* DOREEN.

She stares at his back, then turns away.

They lie, back to back, covered by ARNOLD's *coat.*

Silence.

DOREEN, *cold, pulls coat further over her.*

ARNOLD n*ow partially uncovered, pulls it back.*

DOREEN *partially uncovered, again pulls at the coat.*

The battle for 'coat cover' continues some moments with each player employing more subtle techniques. ARNOLD *after a while, gives up, gets up, impatiently switches on lamp.*

ARNOLD: We won't get back to sleep now. Bloody hopeless.

DOREEN: (*Watching* ARNOLD *move towards umbrella stands.*) Oh, don't tell me you're using your umbrella stand *again.*

ARNOLD: No, I'm not.

DOREEN: What are you doing, then?

ARNOLD: (*Stands over umbrella stand, back to audience.*) Using yours.

DOREEN: (*Appalled.*) Using mine?

ARNOLD: Yours is empty.

DOREEN: Of course it's empty. There's such a thing as having some self-control.

ARNOLD: (*Stands as before.*) Nature calls. Nature calls and must be obeyed.

DOREEN: Do you *have* to use mine?

ARNOLD: (*Half turns towards her.*) Mine's full to the brim.

DOREEN: Can't you hold on?

ARNOLD: What?

DOREEN: Like *I'm* holding on?

ARNOLD. (*Sharp, turns fully towards her.*) No, I can't. For Godsake, there's no prize, Doreen, for having the cleanest piss pot in town.

Oh, sorry (*Bows towards umbrella stands.*) umbrella stand.

Bone bloody china.

(*As DOREEN covers her ears with her hands.*) That's the best thing, yes, cover your ears.

Pause.

ARNOLD *turns, stands again over umbrella stand.*

DOREEN *sits, wincing, covering her ears.*

After some moments, ARNOLD, *relieved, turns back to* DOREEN.

Okay dear, you can uncover them, now.

(*Louder.*) I said, you can uncover them, now.

DOREEN *uncovers her ears.*

We won't get back to sleep, now.

What a night. Now I've got a stinking rotten headache as well.

Have you got any aspirins?

DOREEN: (*Points vaguely behind.*) There might be some in my bag.

ARNOLD: (*Looks around.*) Your bag ...

DOREEN: It's there on the chair.

ARNOLD: (*Searches.*) It is not on the chair. (*Impatient.*) It is *not* on the chair.

DOREEN: Somewhere there. (*Sweetly.*) Just seek and you'll find.

Pause.

Have you found it?

ARNOLD: (*Searching inside bag.*) I've found it.

DOREEN: (*Impatient, as he rummages.*) What are you doing?

ARNOLD: How many compartments has this bloody bag got?

DOREEN: (*Gets to her feet.*) Give it here. Just give it me. Give it to me.

ARNOLD: (*Takes out a new pair of sexy red panties from bag.*) What are these?

DOREEN: They're ... for you. I bought them this morning.

ARNOLD: You've bought them for me?

DOREEN: I thought they might ... turn you on.

ARNOLD: Turn me on?

DOREEN: I just thought ... if I wore them with stockings ...

ARNOLD: Hello. (*Takes out a large tube of cream.*) Is this for me too?

Pause.

DOREEN, sheepish, takes bag with panties and cream in it, places bag on sofa bed.

DOREEN: I just thought you might try it.

ARNOLD: Oh did you?

DOREEN: Well, yes. I've been told it works wonders.

ARNOLD: Who told you?

DOREEN: Well, Anne …

ARNOLD: You've discussed me with Anne?

DOREEN: Of course I haven't. She just happened to say it worked wonders for Tom.

ARNOLD: Did she now?

DOREEN: Said it gave him a new lease of life.

(*Sheepish small chuckle.*) He was quite … quite rampant.

She couldn't keep him off.

ARNOLD: You're pathetic. You know that? Absolutely pathetic.

You think you can go out, buy some stupid cream and hey presto! Then everything's hunky dory!

DOREEN: I just thought it might help.

ARNOLD: Well, it won't bloody help!

DOREEN: You don't know 'til you try it. How can you know?

The *Daily Mail* says it's helped thousands of men.

ARNOLD: It won't bloody help because nothing can help!

(*Turns away.*) Why can't … you just leave it alone?

Pause.

ARNOLD *stands, his back to her, facing front.*

DOREEN: How do you mean, then? Nothing can help?

Pause.

What do you mean?

Pause.

What are you telling me? What are you saying?

Pause.

What do you mean?

Pause.

They've done all the tests. Haven't they done all the tests?

They've done all the tests and said everything's fine.

You told me they said that everything's fine.

Pause.

So what do you mean?

Pause.

Well, I'm sorry for wanting a bit of affection.

A bit of affection. Now and again.

I remember a time when I couldn't keep you off. When you wanted to make love. Morning and night.

I remember a time when you found me attractive!

ARNOLD: (*Half turns towards her.*) Still ... (*Turns away again, faces front.*) do.

Pause.

ARNOLD *stands, back to her. He quickly wipes a tear.*

DOREEN, *unaware of this, turns away towards rear.*

She stops, observes an old record player, casually lifts its lid.

Pause.

DOREEN: (*More to herself.*) God. Look at this. An old record player.

Who in their right mind would want to buy this?

Can't believe there's a market for this sort of rubbish.

Still ... what do I know? He must think there is.

(*Looks closer.*) There's a record on it, would you believe?

Could play it. It's plugged in. (*Turns briefly to* ARNOLD.) There's an idea.

If it works and we blast it out loud, we might, well ... gotta be worth a try.

Pause.

DOREEN *switches on record player, plays the record.*

Glen Miller's Pennsylvania 65000. *She listens a moment. Snaps her fingers.*

Sings the chorus line. Starts to dance. ARNOLD *turns, watches.*

She dances towards him. He stands. Dancing, she looks at him, shrugs.

She takes his hands, places them firmly on her hips.

She places her hands on his shoulders. They stand.

They begin to dance, quite slowly at first, then faster, with a certain panache.

The needle sticks halfway through the piece.

DOREEN *turns the record player off.*

Pause.

That brought back some memories. One or two, eh?

The Palais. The Ritz. The Tower Ballroom, too.

I think that was my favourite. You couldn't beat The Tower.

The atmosphere there was magic. Unique.

ARNOLD: We only went twice. Do you realise that? Both times we were there on holiday. (*Fondly.*) Yes. The North End Hotel ...

DOREEN: You proposed to me there.

ARNOLD: We made ... made love *there*. For the first time.

(*Small chuckle.*) Then worried I might have made you pregnant.

DOREEN: Chance would have been a fine thing.

Pause.

ARNOLD: We could have adopted ... if we'd wanted. *Really* wanted.

We could have done that.

DOREEN: Do you ever wonder ...

ARNOLD: Wonder what?

DOREEN: What it would have been like? I mean ... with a child?

Oh, I know there's no point, but sometimes, I do. I do.

Do wonder. Sometimes.

Pause.

ARNOLD: (*Softly.*) We're alright as we are.

DOREEN: Are we?

Pause.

I never see you ... out in that shed.

ARNOLD: Do you think ...

DOREEN: What?

ARNOLD: (*Shrugs.*) That cream might, well ...

DOREEN: There's no harm in trying it, is there? No.

(*Enthusiastically.*) And there's other things too.

Other things on the market ...

ARNOLD: (*Briskly interjects.*) Okay I ... get the drift.

Pause.

DOREEN: (*Gently hugs him.*) Most times, all I'm looking for is a cuddle.

That's all I'm after. A cuddle, that's all.

ARNOLD: We could always ...

DOREEN: What?

ARNOLD: Take up dancing again?

DOREEN: Take up dancing?

ARNOLD: Why not? I enjoyed it, just then. We both used to enjoy it.

Why did we stop?

DOREEN: Your bunions.

ARNOLD: Oh yes ... I'd forgotten about them.

DOREEN: Besides, there's nowhere. There's nowhere *to* dance.

ARNOLD: There's the Highgrove Tea Rooms.

DOREEN: The Highgrove Tea Rooms?

ARNOLD: They've started having Tea Dances there.

DOREEN: What? With all the old fogeys?

ARNOLD: We're no spring chickens.

DOREEN: I know. Even so though ...

ARNOLD: (*Shrugs.*) Just an idea ...

DOREEN: You're not serious, are you?

ARNOLD: Just ... just a thought.

DOREEN: What about your bunions, then? What about *them?*

ARNOLD: With these wider new shoes, I daresay I could manage the occasional tango or slow foxtrot.

There's a dance there on Wednesday. We could go along then.

DOREEN: I don't know …

ARNOLD: Make a change …

DOREEN: I suppose it would …

ARNOLD: Of course, if you really don't want to …

DOREEN: No … I didn't say I didn't want to. I never said that.

Never said I didn't want to, did I?

Pause.

Sudden noises heard, off: Doors being unlocked, sliding open.

They both stand, listening.

Pause.

ARNOLD: (*Glances at watch.*) He's here. He's opening.

The silly sod's here. (*Listens.*) That's him.

DOREEN: He's opening up all the small rooms. Thank God!

ARNOLD: (*Fumes.*) What a dickhead!

DOREEN: Now, Arnold, go easy. There's no point in getting into a state. Things could have been worse.

At least he's opening. We weren't even sure of him opening at all. Let's be thankful for that, eh?

Small … small mercies?

ARNOLD *shouts towards the door which still has to be opened.*

ARNOLD: This lamp! Wrap it up! We'll take it!

They stand, hugging gently, staring at the lamp.

Fade.

www.ingramcontent.com/pod-product-compliance
Lightning Source LLC
La Vergne TN
LVHW051713080426
835511LV00017B/2890